Printed in Great Britain
by Amazon

62907798R00071